POETIC MOTIFS' Significance of 9

AN ACCOUNT OF TRANSITIONAL HONESTY

POETIC MOTIFS' Significance of 9

AN ACCOUNT OF TRANSITIONAL HONESTY

BY **KISH ANDES**

Copyright © 2017
by Krishuana Anderson

All rights reserved. No part of this book may be reprinted or reproduced in any form or by any electronic, mechanical, or other means, now known or hereafter invented, including photocopy, recording, and information storage and retrieval, without permission in writing from the author.

ISBN: 978-0-9980148-9-0
Library of Congress Control Number: 2017952192

Designed and Published by:
The Solid Foundation Group, LLC
PO Box 1483
Smyrna, GA 30081
www.TheSolidFoundationGroup.com

Printed in the United States of America

Acknowledgements

Giving honor to God from whom all good orderly direction flows... I'd like to thank my childhood church for pouring into me all that you could on the teachings of faith, love, and forgiveness. I am, as we all are, a continuing Wip or Work in Progress. It seems the work is never done and always under improvement.

To my family (Gipson/Comer's and Anderson/Smith's), both ends are too large to place individual names of everyone; but, none of you are forgotten. I love you completely. Thank you for being incredible examples – both by sunrise and nightfall – of how a family that prays together...stays together.

To all the environments in which I was gifted the opportunity to be molded by, thank you for the experiences and lessons.

To my mother Alice Onebo, thank you for life, and your support through all my changes. You are a pillar of strength and my solid rock.

To my Father David Comer, thank you for passing the teachings. If we can just help somebody...our lives won't be in vain. And to my lovely second mother and mentor, Brenda Comer, I can't express enough my gratitude for you. You pushed me to face my fears and supported me every step of the way. No mountain was high enough. You are a winner!

To my Earth first family, thank you for being a part of my life and showing me what it really means to make it against all odds.

To the members of Mosque 15 who sowed into my journey, I am eternally grateful for the wisdom imparted.

Special thanks to the design team, publishers, distributors, editors, and everyone who has journeyed to love me as I have journeyed to love you. There's always another way, but look what we can do together.

Last, but certainly not least... I'd like to thank each and every one of you holding this book. I hope you are encouraged, renewed, and entertained by the words that await you. If you've ever lost your fire and zest to pain and confusion, you know what it means to reconnect with your passion – even when they said you couldn't do it...even when you doubted yourself...even as trials come and the rain continues to pour when all you're fighting for is peace and a smile. Don't ever give up. This race is for you! This one is for US!

Dedications

This book is dedicated to all the lives lost, bruised, and affected by unnecessary violence and crimes of passion. To the Lovers, Artists, Activists, Students, Officials, and Organizers who require strength on their journey fighting for more than worthy causes, I love you.

I offer you a piece of my heart, the audacity to believe we, too, can create change, and the confidence to know your effort and your life is NOT in vain. Weeping may endure for a night...But Joy.

No matter how the world may seek to add, subtract, multiply, or divide us, the Significance of 9, is that through it all, we will ALWAYS return to ourselves...Stronger, Wiser, and Better than before.

Poetic Motifs

A-Chew..1
AmeriKan Oxygen.................................3
Another Black History Poem...................5
Cutie No. 1..6
Calming Water...7
Destined for a Pen..................................8
The Little Things..................................... 9
Monster Hall of Fame Horror
    Story...11
Sapiosexual Wit....................................13
Most Likely To.......................................14
Window Whispers..................................15
The Rise of a Nation............................. 17
My Growing Black Experience............... 18
Scribble.. 20
I Am Krishwana........................ 21
Poet... 23
No Means Yes...................................... 24
Poetic Motifs..25
For Pigment People Looking for Peaches
    When Pep Talks Aren't Enough.........27
Panther Policies................................... 29
Real Art.. 30
I'm a Misfit... 31

Spin Cycle for Groupthink......................... 33
Porch Prophecies of a Swindling
   Survivor... 35
The Séance... 38
Roundtables... 39
Tale of the Missing Black Man................. 43
Sweeter the Juice.. 44
When Swallowing Makes It Hard to
   Breathe... 45
He Makes Me "Wrighte"........................... 46
Future Entrepreneur................................... 50
I'll Sleep When I'm Dead........................... 51
Time... 52

The *Significance of 9*....................... 55

I Am Presence.. 58
Letter to My 27-Year Old Self.................. 59
Sandy... 61
The Auspiciousness of Blues.................... 63
The Ritual of Roses..................................... 65
Wasn't Thinking... 67
Time Fades... 72
Opportunity Awaits.................................... 73
Runaway.. 75
Refuge.. 76
Letter to the Editor.................................... 79

POETIC MOTIFS' Significance of 9

A-Chew

What I've learned
is what I am
is yet to be defined.
I can tell you the secrets and uncover
every dark place in my mind.
But it won't help you understand
the time in which I stand,
For I am timeless, wisdom
acquired beyond my age,
And lessons mastered
in spite of this phase.

I am just what I am, whatever that may be.
What I'm sure of, is that anyone
completely sure is a fool.
And what I'm afraid to mention,
Is anyone with great fear
will be sent to detention,
For Freedom is allergic to its opposite.

A-chewww

KISH ANDES

AmeriKan Oxygen

1-way flight to paradise
Gi'me Get'me Gotcha
MaKe your words precise
Write it prop'ly
so we's can understan'ya
No mispel'
on y'ur applaKashun!
man up Kom' o'er here an' ge' ya
edga'Ka$hun Show'n all you's how'ta
make it to va'Ka$hun
In dis her' lan' you got ta wuK
No'bodi givun' ya nu'than' Yur lazy fuK
Gul ben' it o'er, I'm taKin'
ALL dat Con'fadense an' Strenth',
I'ma call'it addatood'
MaKe a new lash to whip ya wit'
Free yer saY?
Uh hun, well wher' bout's ya staY?
O'er the hill wher' I sen's my whor's home Dat 'der darK matter
feels good on deez heur' bones, Seen it on that Tele'tube
Kash Keep Inticin Youuu
So ya cee, she's invitin meee
I'm 'posed to have all of 'dat It's meye' whuits'premacee'
Ya wood'nta Known Nu'than If it wundn't fa Me.

Breathe in this feelin' AmeriKan,
AmeriKan Oyxgen
Whoa 'O
Kom sweat fa a NiKel an'a dime
We Kill, to Buil'a Empire
Whoa 'O
Breathe in this feelin..
AmeriKan, AmeriKan Oxygen

Another Black History Poem

I can't stand for another story
out of those whack ass history books.
The way that I tell it has never been written.
I refuse to write the facts that you can read.
A lazy learner is meant to burn with questions.
But if I may suggest this...
You may think it's reckless,
But I know it's my best and...
I'm giving it all to you.
The world has been tainted
with Black Face,
The painting of images swimming
with ninjas destroying the vision
and painting me bitter.
It's He-Say, but what do You say?
Cause I will confess the beauty of
Mess. Langston will share
that it's no crystal stair,
But we will keep
climbing to victory.
Yes, me, by daily defining...
I am Beast!
Striving for greatness, I am Free.
Backed by blackness....
New History Speaks!

Cutie No. 1

Pain is temporary
It will Fade...
But the sting of Lack,
Will Permanently Bruise
The Spirit of a Slave

Calming Water

Brenda's daughter
David's Baby
Though Alice made me
It was the blood that saved she
And prepared him for we
I write
He plays
They say
On this day
If peace could take
A piece of cake
I'd give velvet
To more than a wake
Awake you shall Be
Blessed is he that worships
When all is blue
And heavy souls become new
You
Are
So....
Authentically you.

Destined for a Pen

Somehow...
I am heaven for the heavy-hearted

Somewhere...
Someone is in need of a good word.

The kind that seeps between the creeks
of righteous indignities
and classified soliloquys
of dastardly deeds.

Because by my pen,
We are free.

The Little Things

What is this thing that excites my soul
and puts my worries to rest?
More complicated and challenging
than a beginner playing the master at chess,
So silent in the presence yet loudly calling out to me,
Needing my help, and wanting for me
All with an appeal of mastery.
We don't use the same slang...
but you speak to me like none other.
This suits me fine because we find new ways
to communicate with each other.
More than the regular hello or goodbye,
sometimes we use pictures or point to signs.

Tell me what it may be, or could be,
no should be in the future.
I fantasize about what I would do to ya.
I am your Queen and you are my King
My every wish is your command and
I am satisfied with the little things.

Monster Hall of Fame Horror Story

He was my best friend. I never expected anyone to stay. I made a commitment to God very early. And I meant it. So, I got used to people coming and going. Boys and men often showed up in my life wondering what was so attractive about my joy. They could see the light shining through the windows of my soul, so it seemed they stood on the other side of the glass just wondering how hard it would be to shatter it. One day he knocked on my door, when I opened it, he stood before me with balloons and candy. Wanted to wish me a happy birthday he says. Someone in the neighborhood told him it was today. I smiled politely and thanked him. He stood there a little while as if he was expecting me to invite him in…. Instead, I told him the balloons were a nice gesture, I appreciated his efforts but I'm sure there is a little girl less fortunate than I that would probably enjoy them a lot more. He paused at my response and said, "So you aren't going to take them?"

I replied, "No. I don't take candy from strangers or Balloons from Boys because they both have one thing in common that I can't afford."

He said, "Oh really? And what's that?"

I took a step back inside my foyer, leaned further out the door and got right in his face so he could smell my freshly brushed teeth as I said "Tricks, cause I know I'm the only real treat."

Day after day he returned... He returned talking to me about music, poetry, fashion, and doing the most ridiculous things known to man to get my attention. He gained my trust... the way no one else could. He stayed. Every time I asked him to leave, and left... every time I begged him to stay. He was a big bowl of tricks just as I suspected. What I didn't suspect, is that I would like them. The rest of our relationship played out much like a Bad Halloween Film... "Trick, or Treat" What will it be today? That monster won't pick up the phone. I'm calling and I'm crying and I'm stomping and I have, to stop, this, before this baby, makes me throw up again... He said he'd send money to take care of it, and he did. But who's going to take care of Me? I used to be so sweet, guess that's why they give the "tricks" all the names of my favorite treats...

Sincerely,
Candy

Sapiosexual Wit

He used to write me love
poems
With powerful critiques
of the language that dances
between teeth.

What a treat...

To have someone so curious,
About the mysteries
surrounding my character,
that they simply make up shit!

Call back to back, itching
for another taste of this
sapiosexual wit.

I always knew my power wasn't
born in my clit.

Most Likely To

I've been voted too often
"most likely to incite a revolution."

I've worked very hard
at being under the radar...

And here you come,
looking for my pain.

Guess I've only myself
to blame
for the piece I chose
to share with you...
So, pick a safe word,
and let me know
when it becomes too much.

Window Whispers

As the sun peeks its rays above the horizon,
a little girl clings to her steering wheel in tears...
questioning God and explaining her fears...
A cool breeze covers her neck with chills...
as the wind whispers through her ears.

Just keep living.
Just keep loving.
Just keep growing...
Just keep going.

Give me a chance to prove to you that I'm real.
That I'm here.
And what I have is everywhere in the world
But the way I do it to you...
Has never been done before....
And it won't happen again.

You're already perfect.
It's all worth it.
I deemed you worthy...
And I did it on Purpose.
It will all be golden...
you are my chosen.

The Rise of a Nation

There will be no dying
We will simply beat you at your own game
Manipulating your rules
While constructing our own laws.
Busy building a Nation in this hate infested situation.
Where the last really ARE 1st
Since the 1st were the last to steal their way to the Top.
The Auction Block Never Stopped.
But We Will...
And Rise.

My Growing Black Experience

Me? They say...
Of or involving an obsessive interest in one's own satisfaction.
Experience...?
Ok, that's like knowledge or practical wisdom
gained from what I have
observed, encountered, or undergone,
and I know I can't wait to sing THAT song.

Corporate - like a united group of persons
State – the condition of matter with respect to structure.
Existence – The state or fact of Being...
Be...ing hummm...

Being. Yes.

They said I am Black, so lacking hue and brightness,
that I'm absorbing light without Reflecting
any of the rays composing it.

Funny...
how I can see my reflection being knocked off by them.
Enveloped in darkness... pertaining and belonging
to the various populations characterized by
Dark skin pigmentation...
specifically the people of Africa.
American – of or pertaining to
the inhabitants of the United States...

The aboriginal Indians of North and South America
Regarded as being of Asian ancestry and marked
generally by reddish to brownish skin,
Black hair, dark eyes, and prominent...
cheekbones.

Not Blacks. Smh...

Really Webster?!?

What's up with that????

Scribble

There's something so soothing about the task at hand
Sharing stories without judgment is a blast for my pen
Fragile, you felt, telling me about your past
Secrets of the full history can inadvertently destroy the mystery
So I scribble on notebook paper
Like blissful moments of breathing fresh air
You pay no mind to a stranger's glare
You're secure in knowing that I care

I Am Krishuana

See, I'm a cool complication of a fractioned whole...
Stole from a land of rhythm and gold,
Stood on the auction block without a top and Sooooooooold
to the gentleman in the back with the black hat.
See I have come and come again...
A spiritual battle with a savory end...
Died and fought until the WIN...
Cursed and cursed the Master's Inn...
And my bloody battle history has only just begun to be told.
See, I've been uncomfortably abused
And Unrighteous-ly accused of being
worthlessly fit to use for my jewels...
Which I have no right to refuse to bring?
After all...Sex is, Why it's but a thing...
But you see, throughout all my past pain, I sing
Not shame... But Reign Over my created confidence.
Dominion, over my selected ambiance,
Whipped by commercial looks,
Disfigured in commercial books,
And tainted by commercial hooks...
I still choose Me.
No, I will not straighten my hair.
You couldn't pay me to starve myself.
Lotus flower of a woman you may think I'm absurd...
But be still...

For I have founded the herbs to yet another remedy.
Draw near to thee, whether cleared by me of steering clear of me, seek clarity and not conformity...

For I am Black... And I Am a Woman
Freed by the pain of now peaceful souls
You've made me strong so I will be bold.
I AM Krishuana.

Poet

Position
of
Eternal
Truths....

Whichever platform you choose.

Paint
the
Picture.

Tell
the
Truth.

No Means Yes

Paralyzed in a daze,
These days pass so suddenly,
Avoiding the unknown,
Southern comforts of home
Stay Blowing Me...
The Vapors Keep me faded,
Still I'm the one that's waiting
On the inevitability of Fate
to pass through these grains
of sand and get under and
between my toes.
Now my No's sound like yes to
you. And when I say I won't,
you find pleasure in reminding me of what I'll be forced
to do. Resistance makes you want to pull my hair and push
my face in the dirt. Just a different day, bloody dress, same hurt.

As I wash my face...
what stings are the memories of my lost dreams.
Awakening to the dread of lack...
I heard a small voice whisper....
Patience, grasshopper. One day, we'll get it all Back.

Poetic Motifs

On this day I'm firm in what I believe
Even if that means flowing casually
in the shadows of my poetic motifs,
Give way to principles with fluidity
my structure is strikingly familiar
to that of a pilgrim passing Plymouth
no pirate turns down silver
Except when its for Gold!

So, on this day I'm firm in what I believe
Even if that means flowing casually
in the shadows of my poetic motifs.

Put it all in the air like my story was meant to be told
I'll boldly go before the throne...
consciously admitting songs...
actively deciding bright
while juxtaposing trees and life.

Therefore, on this day I'm firm in what I believe.
Even if that means flowing casually
in the shadows of my poetic motifs.

They say those who can... DO
And those who quit... Teach
Well, DO this, reach
up through your esophagus and scrape my ass off yo' teeth!!

I know you didn't mean it.
That's why This lesson I Chose to Preach.

So yes, I'll join you in your vows of silence
breathing out the fear of violence
whispers hiss this vision still...
My freedom shows up dressed to kill.

Cuz on this day I'm firm in what I believe
Even if that means flowing casually
in the shadows of my poetic motifs.

For Pigment People Looking for Peaches When Pep Talks Aren't Enough

Teach us how to love...
Teach us how to sacrifice our all desiring flesh
For your perfect and Holy Will
Teach us how to speak these words...

I'll study your surah's
until it hurts in the worst way
I know you'll pave the way,
and save the day
Forever light my path
while we reach to outlast
The very things that tear
at our souls and
Keep our dreams on hold
Lighten our load...
As we pass this burden on to you.

I free write and write freely
Send the ones who need me

Make my rhythm my life
And our mother's their wife.

Make This place, the one where we stay
And This air, the oxygen we breathe
And This moment... the one that we need...

To be Free

You are knowing... so you know it can be rough
For pigment people looking for peaches
when the pep talks... just aren't enough.

The Panther Policies of Political Weather

Only if…..

This Election is a close one
Between poor black men
None of them are unfair
Nobody loses to cheaters because
The bad men never win
And that great White House is filled
With colorful people of pure descent
None brown with white in 'em
Or Yellow with brown in 'em
None chocolate with almond eyes
Or Vanilla with kinky hair
No one nightmares of equality unequal
And everyone is 5/5ths of a person
Devoid of Alienism
My country is the land of the free
And the home of the brave
Where Capitalism is known for her
Heart and not her brain

Real Art

Real art...
Meant to Inspire Action
Is required to be Acted Upon
So, We Happen.
Beyond our understanding or Agreement
With situations and circumstances.
We circumvent them.
Devoted to a power
Higher than eyes will Meet.
I close all mine... 1,2,3.
Even with you standing here....
I must pretend that I can't see.

I'm A Misfit, Candle-Burning, Pop-Singing, Poetry-Slamming Thick Chick

I'm fine with how you talk.
I just see through it.
Been there... yes, no, maybe,
can't say, could be...
Those are all fine answers
when you are free.
I won't offer you these
chains if you refuse
to promise me wings.
And there's no-thing
that no-man HAS
That will KEEP me on my knees.
I may question, I Can beg,
My case, I will plead.

but never have I ever....
lasted a lifetime either.
It sounds pretty. I do my best.
But, who knows right?

Can you really confirm that you see your life...
with me? the one you don't know?
too much to sow on pillow
that doesn't glow when you throw it.

I'm a misfit,
candle-burning,
pop-singing,
poetry-slamming
thick chick.

I get this, but check this, you will or you won't,
you do or you don't.
No blurred lines...

You don't get to play with my heart
for ANY infinite amount of time.
So, Piss Sir! Or get off the Pot.
There's other men standing at my window
throwing those same damn rocks.

Don't be Selfish now...
Don't do that.

Spin Cycle for Groupthink

It hurts him to walk,
But he doesn't have the car he wants.
It destroys her to be alone,
But she doesn't have the love she wants.
Crazy how peer pressure stings,
When you don't share the Jones' Dream.
But you're perpetually judged by your lack of the Jones' things.
And every time you realize,
You're stuck on spin cycle for groupthink.

We all want a nice car, nice house, 2.5 kids and a dog.
Nice house, nice car, 2 kids and 2 cats.
Nice kids, decent car, bad dog who ate the bird.
Isn't it sort-of strange how we
All repeat the same words?

Like...

I'm afraid to be alone,
I'm about to lose my mind,
I'm late for work again,
That's just Colored People's time.

So, if they can have their own time,
Why don't they have their own acceptance?
Like Being colorful is so outside of society,
That it deserves its own identity.

Cause surely nobody can relate to that?!

Right?

Insanity!!

Porch Prophecies of a Swindling Survivor

This morning
I feel overwhelmed,
With the stress of being
too smart to make the
common choice,
Too dumb to see
the value in nor-mal-cy,
And too strange
to paint a perfect picture
instead of my reality.

So, what's real?

As the world turns
and desire burns
Where do the wounded
find time to heal?
Me with all my willpower,
I pick up and push
through… counting the hour.

Steady being devoured without hope

And ill regard to my smoking...
Picking up that soaking washcloth
to ring out the extra juices
I've found no usage for...

But Pain

Holding this all in and standing the rain, I cry tears of
Frustrated women around the world with vices that
Were born in times of surviving abuse and
Great habits that were instilled
in the innocence of an optimistic truth,
Yet conflicting contradictions
of the contrite and conceited.

What are we breeding?

Ass backwards ideologies and Religious philosophies
that become a whole lot less black and white
When you add some life and stir up the nationalities...

Pop culture is the way to eternal life...
SIKKKKKKKKKKKKKEEEE!
I meant strife, no, no, that's still not right.
See I'm just a little mixed up.
They say 3/5ths of a Human
So, it shouldn't shock you that I chose...

Being over Belonging.
"Yes, Sister Krishuana, we can see that you don't believe,
But just put your faith in this basket,
Keep your eyes on me,
Reserve your doubts for the casket,
This has been proven."

Every man will have a chance to choose,
At that moment, you'll conform
Or sing the blues.

I avoid your sun-day like the plague
Praying God will find another way….

To reach me

As I ride out in the night,
on a mission to keep these rhymes tight.

The Séance

Jesus walks.
But the devil dances in the pale moon light.
We lost sight of my angels
Fighting demons of the night.

Roundtables of Discussions

There's suffering all over the world, yet greed has no face,
There's people all over the world, yet we have a superior race?
There's issues that ain't been solved
but every day brings a new problem.
There's roundtables of discussions...
but no one person wants to solve them.

I wanna know where she is,
the next extraordinary woman who respects herself,
Who wakes up in the morning
and looks to heaven just to dress herself.

See she's not clothed in the latest fashions
Mr. TV told her looked nice;
But, the next expression of freedom that says
she knows she was bought with a price.
She wants more outta life...
Than the next high the club provides.
If she's smart she knows
that high leads to a quick goodbye.
Easy come, easy go, nice place, nice show,
poor planning, poor product,
conjured at the latest Starbucks.

There's suffering all over the world, yet greed has no face.
There's people all over the world, yet we have a superior race?
There's issues that ain't been solved
but every day brings a new problem.
There's roundtables of discussions...
but no one person wants to solve them.

I'm holding auditions for the next rap star
whose alias isn't being a trap star.
See, he knows the struggles of the hood
that's why he fights to be understood.
He knows the power of his words, all the joys and the hurts,
He's been called worthless and dirty
and told he'd never amount to nothing,
So, with music in his heart
he took his guns and started BUSTING,

Tables... At the Waffle House around the corner
And he's been dreaming,
working and hurting until he's just about torn up and...

There's suffering all over the world, yet greed has no face.
There's people all over the world, yet we have a superior race?
There's issues that ain't been solved
but every day brings a problem.
There's roundtables of discussions...
but no one person wants to solve them.

There's hardworking mothers in Africa
who lack the privilege to phone home.
But at 13 he cried when you didn't get him the new iPhone.
And at 17 she whined, cause what she got
Ain't what she thinks she's fly enough to be driving,
And at 30, girlfriend on hip,
he's still forcing his mama be his provider.

When does it end? And when does the revolution begin?
Where's the next family of Kings
that survived the traps of Queens
And headed to Manhattan
So, they can Make it happen....

For all of us? Cuz you see,

There's suffering all over the world, yet greed has no face.
There's people all over the world, yet we have a superior race?
There's issues that ain't been solved
but every day brings a new problem.
There's roundtables of discussions...
but no one person wants to solve them.

Tale of the Missing Black Man

The Enemy knocks on my door but I will not open
He sounds off on my phone but I will not answer
So, speak to me through this spoken word
If the world should find me absurd.

Cuddled next to my pen....
Healing Me... without You.

He says I always leave him for the "bad me"...
I ask, just what makes you think you deserves my Goodies?
When no matter how great of a woman I may be...
You Still force me, to be Here,
without you.

Sweeter the Juice

If I told you I could see your soul
and I had what it takes to put it to rest...
Would you throw away your fears and give me your best?
Cuz I'm deeper, and sweeter, and purer
than any substance you've ever tasted.
Righteousness, don't waste it.
Stick your face in it,
And I'll transform your space
in a way that'll make you wish
Being recognizable was disguisable.
Your vulnerability will crave every inch of me.
What they won't say is why they kept you away,
They told you it was the sin in me,
But the truth is, the only way you win...
Is with Me.
See it's quite spiritually seductive,
Cause we live in a world where
we cum without judgment,
And you never leave without hugging,
Cause your heart can't take the
tugging of the juice.
And just between... me and you....
This is all that's truly Special...
Sweeter the Juice

When Swallowing Makes It Hard to Breath

In my throat, lives a lump,
I thirst...
Your glass is always half Empty and Full
So, I want to Feel you UP!
I am locked out of heaven
when you are inaccessible to me.
Access... Is pure torturous Joy.
Pure because you are.
Torture because I desire to possess it...
Or you...Yea, Both.

He Makes Me "Wrighte"

As I sit here wondering how to start this poem,
I remembered the title and it spoke to me.
Walked me past every insecurity
that never was quite secure in me.
Yet, it's fueling me...
Pushing me past the point of desire.
I aspire to be inspired by he who spits great fire,
And can rewire the inner workings of my intelligence.
Meanwhile, I've just gotta get in and tell this gent, new friend...

Someone in the garden encouraged me to take a bite.
But you wrote with your eyes a survey on life,
And I saw this man giving out the gift of sight,
So, I waited, exhaled, and allowed him...
because he makes me Wrighte.

So, you see, this is a replay,
Cause I wanna be wherever you stay,
That way, no day will come to tear us apart.
I'll say, you're so embedded in my heart,
That you rebuke the "Hell"
out of those places that were so dark,
And gave me a new start and
made me someee kind of shark.

You see, I used to write stories of loves wronged,
But there'll be one less blue-bird singing some sad song today.
You're like that rock
In a hard place
Desperately trying to erase
All the boyish mistakes you made
When becoming your own man,
Still I'm so excited about this grown man,
Who for once doesn't feel like the wrong man,
Singing rap songs about some strong man
Walking on Money but wearing a boy's uniform, Yessss!!!!
I shall overcome,
All the labels they have set out to place on me.
I will embrace the grace he has set out for me.

Open my eyes... So, I can simply See...
Love, and Live Life More abundantly.

He sounds like a prototype,
And, man, this is tough,
Can I really stand next to this giant
Who's no longer just a diamond in the rough?

This dude is smooth and quick and he has all the right stuff.
No, I never said he was an Angel.

I ain't looking for a Savior
I already know the Son.
I'm just really particular about this one,
Because I admire his choices...

Yes, I've heard many voices that have been given the gift of gab,
And they dressed it up on a platter and proceeded to Serve me
a slab only,

I don't eat pork.
It's too tough for my digestive system, so I,
Flipped them and dismissed them
With a... quick kiss to their Ego,

Cause see he knows
I put on a Great Show!
Leave my all on this stage, 'cause I rock crowds, Joe.

Superwoman wit' an extra cape and
I'm a great escape,
But I still bleed yo...

Shit, eat, and sleep
Like the next one.

So, when I'm alone and need a shoulder to cry on
He doesn't write me off as having She-motions
No, he slows down,
Takes his time,
And rights my wrongs by confirming
That my E-motions are valid.
So, I can take out the pride of life and
Just have pride in life,
Acknowledging that I am blessed
Simply because I know him.

New Friend,
Someone in the garden encouraged me to take a bite.
But you wrote with your eyes a survey on life,
And I saw this man giving out the gift of sight,
So, I waited, exhaled, and allowed him...

because he makes me Wrighte.

Future Entrepreneur

"Hi, uhhhh Krish... help me out please. I don't wanna get that wrong."

(frenetic symbol)
Kri-shaun-a

"Oh, ok. That's pretty. And different, well...nice to meet you. Anyway, I'm Abby!

So, tell me about yourself... what do you do?"

Nice to meet you Abby, I'm an entrepreneur.

"Oh wonderful, what line of business?"
Still working on that.

"Well what makes you passionate about your ability to sell?"
Haven't decided yet.

"Ok... so what you're saying is you're currently a jobless mess."
Yes.

I'll Sleep When I'm Dead

18 days of resistance,
24 hours of productivity.
1 moment of truth,
that my roots
grew out of the
bullshit in me.

Who dares to
stand the test?
Pestilential Prisons
with their bars
around my breast,
Wind in my lungs,
Air on my neck,
Fighting the rest
that threatens
my drive,
Where does it
reside? Is there
a house for
Susie Homemaker?
When's it safe to ride?

Time

Wondering what happens to one
in their future according to their past,
Is it the amount of time you used to do it,
that predicts how long it'll last?
Throughout the years, I've been devious,
not far at all from Mischievous,
In Relationships.

People should relate to each other to form a perfect bond,
that inspires a Composer's song to be more than just notes,
Or a writer's song more than just lyrics...
But, but, beautiful music that tickles the eyes of a pimpett
That releases mighty droplets of laughing tears...
From all the foolish things and pain created and received
throughout the years.
A wise woman once sang, No pain, no gain.
So how can "the Fed" be sane?
It seems by babying the world,
You take away their life,
Cause it's always the woman whose husband fills her with strife
That can stand on the podium and say to the world
I am the best wife!

He has ever had, and he will ever see,
He got his power because of me.

Yet, now he runs after the ones
who ran from him in his time of seek.
They chose to mistreat his dreams
and his goals in their early state.

When I was the one who brought them
to life and pushed them all at full rate.
See it's the moochers just seeking a good life that take the
richest of my pain.

On the surface of my mind and social appearance, it is I who
least gained,
And in the oceans of my mind and walls of my heart,
I know I deserve the fame.
But that's what happens when instead
of taking it to the hoop, You get gamed.

So regardless the time it takes to get there,
Or the few seconds it takes to fall,
the end remains the same...
Time, still unfair, unchanged, and unchained.

The Significance of 9

The most beautiful poem I never wrote,
Used the most beautiful words I never spoke.
Through all the moments I almost choked,
Came healing from beyond the ethers when I was broke.

I brought peace to those who grieved their loved ones.
Over rainy days and missed parades,
I threw shade to those blinded by the light,
Reserved my hate for those who weren't right.
And you could've been anything but what you were,
Still lives beyond red eyes will tend to blur,
But just keep stirring...I'm still merging.

All my needs gave way to yours,
All my keys made clones of hers.
So, if ever the inevitable were to ever exist,
I made sure to provide the inertia for your kiss.

I rock steady, always merry,
Always married to the Beast.
Woke up silent crying giants never screaming for release,
Only begging at my feet.
I serve my city without fail,
Like he served fiends to silence their yells,
And she prescribes relief for those with painkilling needs,
But no one is immune to being stung by bees.
Because we are all susceptible to the "Powers that be".

So, watch, listen, learn, baby yearn
For the Significance of 9
Humanitarian and Equestrian.
Can you hold on and steer the divine?

Cause somebody's running out of time.
And still looking for a sign.
Holding ill contentment, harbored resentment,
Captured in my prose beneath the whoas.
So, I professionally regurgitate your support.
Giving back all that which you abort.
Avoiding all the slack that you adored...
Funny how good it felt to believe I was Yours.

But we both know,
I am service to mankind
Not even I will truly own
The Significance of 9

So, Love the Divine
Build your own shrine
But share the significance with
All discerning wise ties.

I returned to myself as if I never left.

I Am Presence

Therefore, I am presently awakening to Being,
While simultaneously deadening to thinking,
When we meet, I hope to be greeted by your Essence,
When we speak, I hope it's not of your fears, or your blessings.
For every soul learns,
And every heart will burn.
Though every soul has the potential for scolding,
Life provides the platform for every soul's molding...
Into shape, and out of form
Back through time, to carry on.
So, when we dance,
Our flesh will move,
But only in presence can we groove.

Letter to My 27-Year Old Self

Dear Kish,

Stop and smell the roses a little.
No need to hurry If you can see all that we've become,
You'll enjoy every precious and sacred moment
of free time you have.

After 60 you will travel so much
and experience so much power and freedom,
Some days will make you cry for a boob
wishing you didn't have to be in charge of THAT call.
But they go a lot easier on us in our older age.
Peoples' opinions just don't matter
as much after the kids are grown.

After 60, we take this sweet old body
to a few nude beaches and join the rest of the
freaks on whatever island we choose.
Showing off after menopause,
Hot flashes come and it makes you wonder
why you ever complained
that you were cold natured at all.

Please pursue more knowledge of yourself...
Really puts the world in perspective
when you know where you stand in it.
People are looking for leaders just as they always have.
Go full force with your art.

Give it your heart and continue
pushing right towards freedom.
You will find your power again
in your process of weeding
out the undesirables.
As always Self, I love
you much.

Can't wait til
we collide in
this parallel
Universe.

Sandy

I remember the way her hug felt
The first moment that I almost pushed past her,
The pretty face of the Betty Boop granny
with the beautiful gray fro.
If you thought that was beautiful in her youth,
Wait 'til you hear her speak.

I saw some of the most beautifully pure skin
I have ever seen on a woman,
Her hair didn't fit a fashion so expressive
that you could no longer tell what it was,
Instead, quite peacefully she had decided,
that this will be It for today.

I remember...

Her Patience with me as I gathered
my emotional bags of mess,
The way she sat quietly as I rambled
and fumbled through my healing.
She adjusted my vibrations as she frequented
my frequency so frequently,
That I speak of her sequentially and intentionally.

The magnitude of love I felt
surrounding me in her squeeze.

I Met my Mother....
Over and Over and Over...
until she was Me.

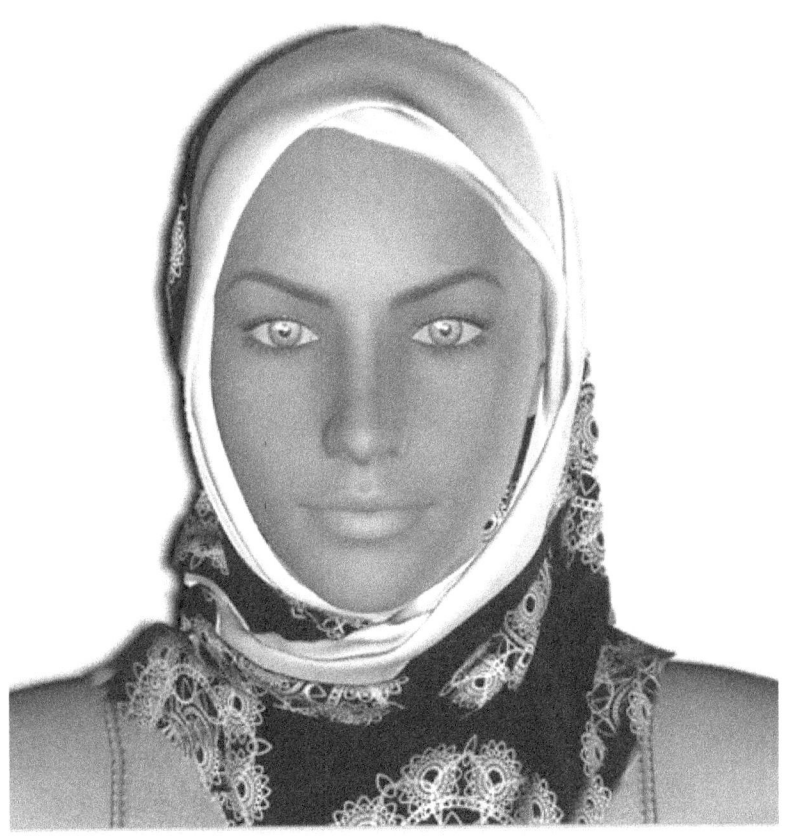

The Auspiciousness of Blues

Today I wrote life
When you preached death
Today I became a star
When you asked who's next
When stumbling occurs
And you haven't a word
And you've bowed before a throne
But Grace all is gone

When your clothes are all dirty
And they've misplaced their mercy
When the auction blocks atop
And police brutality doesn't stop
When all the people riot
And the children hide in silence
When death comes for your brother
And teardrops haunt your mother
When Joy neglects your morning
And the sun disrupts your storming
Only you can change perspectives
On what happens to your next years
As for me, I won't stop a second
Every test will teach a lesson
For no one is immune
When the fat lady sings her tune

The Ritual of Roses

I'm worried about you
But something tells me
You've worried too
And I think she's worried
Enough for the both of us;

But I'll never blame her for that
Cause Loss...is tough
So, I can't lose you
I'll never choose to

Even if we lose...
I will always love you.

The ritual of beautiful roses is growth, and then display
But all love will grow
And all beauty will wither away
Semblance will meet symmetry
So, I'll meet you at the cemetery
Immortalized in Memory
No dead rose....
Can take your love from me

Wasn't Thinking

She wasn't thinking,
so, it was easy for her to start sinking at every word he spilt,
And every time he ought to tilt her head and neck,
Plus, he always had Kush on deck.

Every sign pointed to it being time to go, time to show him
She was too precious to be played with and left broken down
at the silence in place of the sounds her phone made.
Ringing off the chain about every rave
She fell silent as her heart rate sped up
Wishing she could choke the truth out this pregnancy test

Cause not I, she, we, no hold up...
we weren't thinking...

Well I wasn't thinking, and I know he...
Wasn't thinking he'd be a daddy by next December, in fact,
HE hadn't even remembered to call and check....
She went through murder alone,
holding on to her favorite church song to give her comfort
Jesus loves me, yes, I know, so why didn't she know?
Why did she make the choice to go?
Certainly, she had read that all things work
to the good of those that love Him...
But she couldn't stop thinking of how she had served him...
instead.

Plate of hot food, glass of cold lemonade,
make up sponsored by Mac,
Outfit provided by Victoria's lingerie.
All to hear him say, I'll never leave you, because I love you...
So now she's faced with one set of footprints instead of 3,
Crying out for forgiveness, Father, please don't desert me...

I didn't want to kill my baby.
And for all intents and purposes
if you knew this would hurt so bad...
Why didn't you save me... from myself...?
And now she can't stop her clock from blinking...
waking up in a cold sweat...
trying desperately to rip her heart right out of her chest,
wishing she could turn it into an ugly vest,
hang it up in her closet and WALK AWAY!

But she wasn't thinking...

so, she called him again today.
They weren't thinking words could do the same damage...
They sat across the table and kept
spitting their words of hatred cause at first glance,
It was obvious she lived below the margin,
So, it made her an easy target.
She had been born with a disease called poverty.
No matter how many days she stayed inside,
handwashing her thrift store dress and
Sleeping on top of her mattress to press it,
she never got a 'Yes, it's very nice,'
Or we thought twice, and decided we really like you...
We never worried that you'd throw rocks at us...
And you scooted over first to reveal an empty seat on the bus.
Instead they skipped class to drink wine
in the girl's bathroom at school right before lunch...
Being a little tipsy gave their insults an extra punch.
They had gotten it from
Sheila's drunk auntie that runs the salon
and preaches glamour and money...
After all, only the prettiest girls get all the honey.
They never thought it would go this far,
and they weren't thinking their words
Would push her to cry uncontrollably
on the top of the school building,
Writing her goodbyes and tearing it up again,

figuring nobody would care if she jumped.
All they did was talk about her at lunch,

Though she starved herself, and permed her hair,
and pressed her clothes and stole colognes
and perfumes and she fumed...
What did I ever do to you?? To be so cruel to me?
My only dream... Was you... Accepting me.
See when she was 13... she lost her whole family
and just barely escaped death herself.
But they weren't thinking she was close enough
to worthless to take her last breath.
They weren't thinking she would really cut her wrists,
but now they can't stop thinking of how her life ceases to exist...

He wasn't thinking he'd repeat the cycle,
Never imagined he'd end up stealing cars with Michael,
And becoming the very thing,
he had seen on the screen at Big Ma's house,
He never thought he'd get a rise out
of seeing the fear in little girl's eyes...
Right before he took what they held so dear,
Skipping all four-play only leaning down
to whisper in her ear, if you tell...
I know where your mama lives.
He wasn't thinking he'd wake up one day
and not recognize his own reflection,

Or have lights go out in the middle of the night and
have to seek protection.
He never thought he'd identify with a band of thieves,
Or criticize his girl Latrice for being weak cause she cared,
Weak cause she dared to stay awake,
Weak cause she couldn't break this unshakeable epiphany
That she'd die of heartbreak at his wake.
The Next time he decided at the loss of a dime,
He'd put a gun to another man's head
and threaten to scatter his mind...

He wasn't thinking.

Time Fades

As
Time
Fades
in
Passing,

I'm forced to be reminded
The memory of your propaganda
Makes me wish I had a sandwich.

Opportunity Awaits

Hot summer day on a cold dark night
Tell me where I can spread
these old tattered wings and take flight.
Show me where I leap with bounds,
as joys and sorrows start to mound,
Unforgiving roads that twist and turn,
before me stands desire, and I burn.
Scorned from bruises of misuse,
full with passion for this strange fruit.
Every cycle adds its actions,
laced with promises of satisfaction

I'm overwhelmed by energy I don't use,
Thinking over issues, life after abuse

Where's the hospital for the heavy-hearted?
Why not finish the job you started?
2 fist pumps from a panther-ed party,
Pink panty pull down, times hard, tardy.
Why do they feel like healing and then some,
round bottomed nice lady, take that! Get some!
When our paths cross and it's just you and I...

Will we contemplate the choices
that make us giants in their eyes?
We can choose to build each other up
or tear down paradise gates,
even when love is confusing...
It doesn't make it fake.
It doesn't make it tainted,
when you acknowledge the blur...
we see through the lenses
that dust settles after its stirred...
Rile up the people!
Tell'em I'm where I want to be...

Right here in the middle of loving you and me...
As opportunity awaits.

Runaway

Dear Runaway,

You don't deserve my page.

Refuge

How many times is too many times to run to you?
I hear your voice and I listen,
you call me forth and I come.
You instruct me to do better and I start,
but I stop, and turn around
When trouble does the same thing.

I've been down roads of discovery
that intrigued my intellectual sensibility,
To the point of no return...
Yet, each night I yearn for ignorance so bliss
that it would make a pack of demons feel like being kissed
by an angel, has to be the best thing
Since fried rice.

You've given me style beyond compare
and talents beyond my heir.
A thirst for my heritage and passion for my people
that is already being manifested
In the lives of those around me...
still I cheat myself of your goodness.
Rob me, of your mercy, and Reason
I, out of your grace.
Though amazing she is and sweet she sings,

See I happen to be able to,
See, I think up a few good reasons as to, why, I,
Am not worthy of your Forgiveness.
Thank God there's only one "I" in forgive ...
And that "me", is YoU.

If it wasn't, Lord what would I do to myself
On sleepless nights and horror-filled walks beside Christ,
Where persecution is a requirement
and doubt is at an All-time high?
Being born to a generation of high-rollers
who free their mind by freeing themselves
of the responsibility of you.

So, I find 'Me' out of date
And realize I'm unable to relate
To people who run from you
when You ArE My ReFuGe ...

I can't eat, I barely sleep, it's hard to breathe
Without you in my life,
I need you like Africa needs rice,
Like the Gambler needs dice,
And the sweetest thing born to a woman
HAS to have just a little bit of spice to survive

Cuz I...
Am so in love with you ....
Whatever you want to do...
Is alright with me.

Letter to the Editor

Dear Editor,

What of loving your neighbor as you love yourself?? Sure, I know I'm promised. Sure, I cheated, I broke my promise, I made an exception, I gave it away to the monster who didn't deserve it. In my defense, I went to church every Sunday, just like I was supposed to. I showed up and I purged my soul and begged forgiveness for every tiny little lie, and every time I thought unclean thoughts. I prayed for strength to withstand the test of time and in His word, He said He'd make my enemies my footstool. Instead, my body grew more and more excited with each one of my enemies' moves. Who can defy nature but You?

So, what happens when that line gets blurred? When Friend and Foe are one in the same and in the innocence of my youth I couldn't tell the difference?? Yes, I made the decision; but, my heart only meant to do what I was told. "Be a fisher of men," says the Word... Be everything to everybody.

In order to relate to a criminal in darkness you have to cross a few lines to earn your stripes. He didn't respect me because I was spotless... "what do you know?" he mocked at me. So, I was only hoping to show a few spots in order to be an example of how the Word could make him pure again.

It wasn't until after I became dirty that he was even able to weaken my defenses and break me down to the rags in which he felt. The leper parading as Prince showed me what I knew nothing of. And when I bit that apple, I became aware of my own spots…. But the worst part of all this is that he became aware of them, too. I went from the one who could do no wrong to just another lying woman who couldn't be trusted like all the rest. Wow! What a cruel test.

I was only doing what I was told. Learning to be everything to all men in order to bait them towards the hook… So, what happened with those words? Why didn't you reel me back in when you saw that I had sacrificed myself for your cause and even the rewards I held out for? Why did you allow me to be confused in The Bible's double talk? What purpose did you have for me that was so grand that I couldn't achieve being everything to everybody, just as I was anti-social with the lepers keeping myself spotless for your glory? Surely you saw it wasn't possible to talk and shut up at the same time…

So, you see…. I don't believe this was all my fault. The more words I learned, the more the lines were blurred. The more rules I followed, the more I was susceptible to. Like sit, stay, wait, don't run, loosen up, smoke this, drink that, it's time for some fun. He stayed by my side the way none of those Christian men did. He believed in my cause even though he didn't believe in you. And when I approached him to do the unthinkable, He even cried out for MY soul because He feared your wrath for accepting that gift.

Something I meant in purity was made foul... Who authored the confusion printed where I sought clarity? If you acknowledge where I am, in my defense, don't forget where the desires of my heart were born or where they died... It started with a few words... Promise me your purity. And ended with the same ones... How was I supposed to guard my heart WITH your Word AND against it?

How could the innocence of my youth teach me that being a fisher of men would make THEM my God instead of YOU?

About the Author

Born in Hattiesburg, MS, Krishuana Anderson, also known as Kish Andes, set out on her journey to perfect her craft, writing her first poem at the age of nine.

Inspired by the death of her great grandfather, seeing the pain in her Nana's eyes, she became immediately aware of the power of love and the pain of loss. Very early, she began to question everything about life as it relates to the subject, which lead to what she now realizes is her greatest passion – understanding the intricacies of heart matters.

Since moving to Atlanta at the age of 12, she has performed and directed plays and spoken word shows – both locally in her own community and abroad. She enjoys traveling and studying other cultures through experiencing their Arts' communities. She has received 4 out of 5 Star performance ratings in the Edinburgh, Scotland's Summer Arts Festival and has packed the house for many of her student productions of Black Milk in London England, Medusa, and The Colored Museum in Chicago, IL.

Krishuana has earned a Bachelor of Arts Degree from Columbia College where she is grateful to have been groomed and enhanced on her journey to fine tuning her craft. Her concentration was in Theatre with a minor in Poetry. While there, she held office on the Black Student Union as well as participated in the Reach Out community development program.

The name, Kish, was given to her by one of her close friends that she frequently collaborated with while studying and performing in London. Kish has participated in many open mic events in all the places she frequents and love. Whether it's her written poetic language, rapping or acting, the artistic platform her work has both developed and promoted from is to be the "Voice of the Misunderstood".

Life can be unforgiving; but, the active principles of Love possess a transformative power greater than anything she's ever experienced or studied. So, she remains constantly inspired and motivated to provide representation to the stories and voices that are so often just like hers...simply misunderstood.

ORDER MORE BOOKS
Mail along with payment to: **P.O. Box 1483 Smyrna, GA 30081**

Name

Address

City

State   Zip

Book		Qty	Total
	Poetic Motifs' Significance of 9 by Kish Andes Genre: Poetry Cost: $13.95/each*		$
	How To Fade Like Griffin by Kendrick Henderson Genre: Educational Cost: $15.95/each*		$
	The Cartel's Daughter Unedited: Raw and Uncut! by Carmine Genre: Crime/Thriller/Urban Cost: $14.99/each*		$
	Bullet Proof by Bodie Quinette Genre: Self-Help/Motivational Cost: $15.95/each*		$
	The Pig Who Became President By Alana Johnson Genre: Children's Cost: $12.95/each*		$

![book] *Set Free by Truth* *By Amari Johnson* *Genre: Children's* *Cost: $12.95/each**	_____	$ _____
SHIPPING & HANDLING: *1-3 Books: $5.00* *4-9 Books: $9.00* *$3.95 each addt'l book*	_____	$ _____
TOTAL ENCLOSED		$ _____

Acceptable Forms of Payment: Money orders or U.S. bank issued checks made payable to **The Solid Foundation Group**. Please do not send cash.

Visit our website to learn more about our authors and their books and/or to order online.

www.TheSolidFoundationGroup.com

www.ingramcontent.com/pod-product-compliance
Lightning Source LLC
Chambersburg PA
CBHW052131010526
44113CB00034B/1796